"An inspiring and thought-provoking fast read... perfect for group study and reflection."

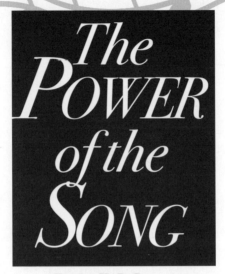

The POWER of the SONG

Tracey H. DeBruyn

The MASTER Teacher®

The MASTER Teacher, Inc.
Publisher
Leadership Lane
P.O. Box 1207
Manhattan, Kansas 66505-1207
Phone 800-669-9633 Fax 800-669-1132
www.masterteacher.com

ISBN 1-58992-149-6
First Printing 2004
Printed in the United States of America

Dedication

This book is dedicated to the many friends and colleagues who offered insights and guidance, but most especially to my husband, Robert L. DeBruyn, who has set the most profound example of leadership I will ever know.

Contents

About the Author

Tracey H. DeBruyn

Tracey DeBruyn is president of The MASTER Teacher, Inc., as well as its two subsidiary companies, Educational Publishers and Professional Mentoring. She is one of America's most insightful and practical writers in education, as well as in business, industry, and the professions. Her work is read and utilized by school administrators and by executives in many corporations, both large and small.

A graduate of Notre Dame, Ms. DeBruyn has an innate ability in public relations, written communication, and management. She serves as a consultant to educators and business people, as well as to lawyers, doctors, and other members of the health care profession. You will find that her thinking and suggestions are exciting, creative, and profound. Her writing zeroes in on the issues facing all who are in leadership positions, separates the wheat from the chaff, and gives you insights that would take many writers volumes to explain.

Ms. DeBruyn is a student, as well as a practitioner, of excellence in management and has insights far ahead of her time. She is the author of *Leadership Vision* and *Professional Vision*, which are continuous programs of professional training read by managers and employees all over the country, and of *Messages from Management*, a guide to over 300 different employee counseling situations. And she is the coauthor of *School Promotion, Publicity, & Public Relations...Nothing But Benefits*.

Prologue

The Power of the Song is the second book in a series written to help leaders of organizations, big and small, grapple with critical issues that their organizations are currently facing or will be facing in the future. The first book, *When the Choir Began to Sing*, is the story of a small church in the town of Midville that is in serious decline. The competition from newer churches cropping up in the area is causing the most faithful members of the Community Church to reexamine what they want their church to be and represent. Reverend Kyle Martin's decision to abandon the old church for a new building ignites the church's most loyal and active members—the choir—to action. The choir members put their heads together and write a powerful new song that is the sentinel act of what eventually becomes a renewed and reinvigorated church.

When the Choir Began to Sing explores the stages that any organization must pass through during periods of significant change. The metaphor of a small-town church supplies readers with the perfect springboard from which to search for the answers to their own organization's dilemmas—including how to nurture the untapped leadership that exists within.

The book ends with a message of hope for all leaders who are on a quest to reignite their organizations. And yet it begs the question—*How?* What are the steps that a leader must take between inspired convictions—and taking the actions that will result in the desired outcome? How does a leader make the message of the organization—its song—become so compelling that strangers to the organization want to hear it and follow it? Is there a prescription that other successful organizations have used to bring new life to their organizations?

The answers to these questions and more are explored in *The Power of the Song.* The book takes the reader back five months to the Sunday afternoon of the debut of the now famous song. And Rev. Kyle Martin is pondering the very hows that every leader on the brink of a great challenge asks.

The Power
of the Song

Reverend Kyle Martin finally sat down in his study after one of the most surprising days of his short career as a minister.

The congregation had gone wild over the choir's new song and their rendition of it. The words had been moving, of course—though he would have to hear them over and over to truly understand the impact of the choir's message. But it was the passion of the choir's delivery that had been so powerful. He had felt it through his whole body. He hadn't expected to feel it. He wasn't even sure he wanted to.

Up until this morning, Kyle was certain that the only way to revive this church was a new building program. His colleagues in other churches all over town were building things. He, himself, had grown up the son of a contractor, so wanting to build things came naturally for him. The process of building was exciting and was one he enjoyed. But right now he was in a church on the decline, and he hated it. He had been hired to bring Community Church back to its earlier standing in the district. The reality was that this was not a job he was trained for. His schooling was in theology, counseling, and preaching.

He didn't know the first thing about how to make a church grow.

But he did know one thing: While the enthusiasm of today was powerful—unless it was nurtured it would die.

He had learned the hard way that enthusiasm alone was never enough to get you to the finish line. Enthusiasm is impossible to sustain without an attainable goal to shoot for—and a plan of action to get you there.

In his mind, what the church needed—had to have—was more members. This would be the key to new resources, new programming, and a new building.

While deep in thought, a drop of water hit Kyle's head and slid down his cheek. It was raining and the roof was leaking— again.

The rebirth of this church, he thought impatiently, couldn't happen too soon. He had to find a way.

An idea came to him. But—he knew it was a risk.

The Reverend Kyle Martin

Rev. Kyle Martin was a study in contrasts. He actually looked more like an ad for a sporting goods catalog than a minister. He favored flannel shirts and jeans over a shirt and tie any day of the week. When he had to dress more formally because of the requirements of the job, he felt like he was being punished. Dressing up was the one thing he had always disliked about going to church as a boy. But the other things about church were magic to him—always had been.

He loved the feeling he got when the people he cared about got together to do something that was bigger then they were separately. He marveled at the way the various personalities of a small community could be transformed for an hour by one unifying event. He loved the way the sun filtered through the stained glass, making carnival-colored patterns on the floor. And he even liked the smell of burning candles and melting wax.

But it was the music he loved the most. To him, church music was glorious—all the different kinds of it—he loved every one of them. (Well, maybe not the hymns that are sung with so many high notes that nobody can possibly reach them, so most people just mouth the words—except for those few tone-deaf parishioners who don't have the vaguest idea of how bad they sound, so they just bellow out the words anyway.)

Yet, he thought most of the music was beautiful. There wasn't anything like it that gave him the feeling that he went to church to get. The music always made him feel that he could do more and be more. And for a brief period of time after church he always had the resolve to try harder.

That's why he was so determined not to let this moment—this unexpected opportunity that had just been handed to him—slip out of his hands. The magic was there in the song that he had heard today. Most of the magic had gone out of his life when his wife had died three years ago. He had accepted this position to get a new start. But it hadn't been easy.

"I want so much for this congregation," he said to himself, thoughtfully. "This church could be more … a lot more…. How can I keep what I heard today alive? How can I help it thrive?"

To make everything come together would require some very delicate handling of some very forceful personalities, he reflected. Fortunately, he had some experience dealing with difficult personalities. Working around his father's construction sites summer after summer during college and seminary had given him a pretty thick skin and a few ideas that just might work if he played his cards right. The key would be in leading the choir to understand the depth of their commitment.

He only hoped he had the courage to do what he had in mind.

Putting the Plan into Action

Kyle entered the church on Monday afternoon and ran right into Don Wilson, the custodian. Of all the members of the congregation, Kyle perhaps knew Don the best. Don was always at the church long after everyone else had left—cleaning, sweeping, or posting the title of the sermon on the message board outside. Don's work in the church had given the two men many opportunities to simply chew the fat together.

Kyle and Don had come from similar backgrounds—Kyle's father ran construction crews, and Don's father had worked in the steel mills. The language they shared was always simple, direct, and honest. Kyle couldn't exactly call Don a friend since they hadn't actually come close to that level of understanding in all the time they had spent together. But Kyle knew Don was a tough old bird and would be able to handle what he was about to dish out.

"Wasn't that great yesterday?" Don boomed enthusiastically. "I was so excited that I couldn't stop thinking or talking about the service all afternoon and even into the evening. I don't think I've ever had an experience like it in my life!" Don had all the

pride and excitement of a young boy sharing a big, fantastic
secret with a kindred spirit he thought would feel the same way.

"Yes, it was a great day," Kyle replied, and he deliberately
began walking back to his office, as if he intended not to give it
any more thought.

Don looked at the minister in disbelief. Hurrying after him,
Don asked, "Is that all you're gonna say? 'Yes, it was a great
day.' That's it … nothing else?"

"Well, what do you want me to say—that it was the greatest
moment of my life, too? That your song is going to completely
turn this church around?"

"Well, yeah, something like that…. At least that you really
liked it, and that it has the *potential* to turn this place around."

"Well, just singing a song won't turn this place around," Kyle
said soberly. "It was a real feel good experience though—a real
feel good experience…"

Don's anger was starting to build to a boil. He didn't believe in
being disrespectful to a member of the clergy, but this guy was
making him change his mind about that. Come to think of it,
Rev. Kyle hadn't been as supportive as he could have been of
any of their efforts from the very beginning. It seemed to Don
that Rev. Kyle hadn't even been respectful of their traditions or
their history. And now, after all their hard work on the song and
the performance yesterday he wasn't even going to thank them
and give them credit for what they had pulled off?

"What do you mean—'a real feel good experience'?" Don let the words *feel good* spit through the air. "FEEL GOOD! It was a lot more than a feel good experience. We worked hard on those words and on the music itself. We've got something that'll last."

"Well, I agree that you've got something for posterity—for the record books. You've got me on that one," Kyle retorted.

"'For *posterity*'! 'The *record books*'! Are you trying to insult me? I mean … us?" Don was hopping mad now. He wanted to sink his teeth into this man and hurt him badly—the way he, himself, had been hurt by Kyle's words. How could this minister trivialize what he and the choir had done? Their song was no small accomplishment. It was *huge*. Don just *knew* it was. And this excuse for a preacher was not going to stomp all over their accomplishment. "What kind of minister are you anyway?" he blurted out.

"The kind of minister who believes that there is far more potential here than to settle for *one* feel good performance," Kyle responded cagily.

"What are you talking about, man?"

"If you want to find out, get the rest of the choir here for a meeting at seven tonight." Kyle then went into his office and closed the door quietly behind him.

Insight 1: The potential of an organization's song is great, but it is just that—*potential*.

Once an organization finds its "song," it has taken its first step toward greatness. But the song, by itself, is just a series of words artfully arranged. As Rev. Kyle pointed out to Don, a one-time feel good experience can't turn the church around. For an organization to grow, it must sing its song passionately many times to many different audiences. It won't be until the song has been sung hundreds, even thousands of times that people will begin to hear and believe in the power of the words.

Monday Night at Community

Kyle waited in his office, watching the clock count the minutes past seven. It had taken every bit of restraint he could muster not to go in before 7 p.m. Though the tardiness would appear extremely rude on top of the resentments that were already brewing about the way he had responded to Don earlier, he knew he had to let the anger steep. Anger was a powerful emotion. It was even more powerful than the emotion that had empowered the choir to write their song and to give their exemplary performance yesterday. And he knew that only when these very good people could experience strong emotion over losing the momentum that they had built would they become committed to taking the next step.

There were many ways to move the choir to a place of action, but this was one that Kyle was very familiar with. He had seen the union bosses use this strategy countless times to stir up his father's workforce. This time he was going to see that it was used for the purpose of good.

Kyle knew of too many congregations that had stopped and simply patted themselves on the back before they had reached their ultimate goal. Well, not his congregation. Something in the song had really gotten to him. He knew he couldn't allow his congregation to give up. Not this time... Even if it meant that *he* would become the biggest casualty of the church's transformation. He supposed he was a little angry with himself, too—for never risking it all before ... for letting this congregation settle for a lot less than what it could have become.

He decided it was time, and at precisely 7:18 p.m. he walked through the door of the meeting room—and sure enough, he thought to himself, he could have cut the hostility with a knife.

He smiled and apologized for being late. He welcomed everyone and thanked them all for coming.

In the mood they were in, the simmering group of men and women were insulted by his polite and friendly gestures. So before he could get the first words out of his opening statement, Tony Coffman stood and said, "We heard what you said about our performance, that it was 'a real feel good experience.'" Tony had emphasized the words *feel good* precisely the way Don had earlier in the day. "Well, we think it was a lot more than that!"

"Yeah, that's right," Irv Finkbinder piped up. "We think it was a lot more than that!"

Irv had surprised himself by speaking up. He wasn't much of a risk-taker. He loved being a part of the choir, but alone he never felt that he had much going for him. Yet, there was something about the minister's reaction to their song that had really gotten under his skin. In Irv's estimation, their song was one of the best things that had happened in the church in 25 years. This time he wasn't just going to roll over and take it. He and the rest of the choir had worked long and hard on the song. Many of the words were even his. He had a way of making certain words rhyme—and not just in a meaningless or cornball kind of way. No, if he did say so himself, sometimes in an inspired sort of way.

"Explain what you mean Irv," said Kyle, trying to dig deeper. "What do you mean when you say it was a lot more than that?"

"Well, I guess I'm not entirely sure," Irv said slowly and thoughtfully, surprised to be asked to embellish his opinion. "But what I do know is that the song meant something to all of us. And I guess we're ready to put our words into action." The heads of all of the choir members were nodding in agreement.

"Are you sure you're ready?" Kyle queried again.

"We sure are, hot-shot," Tony Coffman yelled out, feeling a lot more confident now within the new atmosphere of resolve of the choir. "And by the way, where are you in all of this? We haven't seen much action out of you lately. Aren't you supposed to be the leader around here? Well, you want *us* to take action, but I think it's high time that you do some powerful leading."

"Yeah, how 'bout you doing some leading?" some of the other members of the choir resounded.

Those were the words Kyle had been waiting for. "I think you're right," he said. And he stood up to begin.

Insight 2: Your most important decision: How will you position yourself as the leader?

You can have good people in an organization without an effective leader, but you can't have a great organization without a proactive leader who is ready, willing, and able to lead.

There are three extremely important decisions every leader must make. The first and most important is: How will you position yourself as the leader? In other words, will you be a leader who will allow things to materialize in their own way, or will you be a leader who will cause things to happen? Will you be a leader who develops the talents of people, or will you allow people to dwell on their own weaknesses and those of others? Will you be a leader who seizes opportunities and makes the most of them, or one who lets opportunities slip by? Will you be one who will settle for a good organization, or will you take the actions necessary to make your organization great?

How you decide to position yourself with those being led is the most important decision you will make. If you don't position yourself to lead, you can't lead.

Promises of Change

Kyle had risen slowly to his full 6-foot-2-inch frame after the choir had said the very words he had been waiting to hear. But he was still not certain that *they* believed what they were telling him to do. He knew that the congregation was anxious for something new and refreshing to happen in the church. Yet, he also knew that when they were challenged to move outside of their comfort zone, they would start to question him and the direction of his leadership. At Community, the freshness came when the choir developed and presented their song to the rest of the congregation. Now Kyle was going to explore just how much they were willing to commit to changing and building their church.

"You say you want me to lead," Kyle began. "It's not only my job to do that, but it's my desire to do that. So that's one promise I will make.

"There are even more important promises I will make to you:

"I promise to help create an environment here where everyone's talents can be utilized to the fullest.

"I promise to listen to you and minister to your individual needs.

"I promise to not let you settle for having less than a great church.

"And I promise to stay here with you to get this done, no matter how rough it gets, until the day you don't want me here anymore."

The silence in the room was deafening. Was this the same man who had belittled their song—who had made them so angry just a few minutes ago? He was a hard one to figure out, that was sure.

"I love your song. But if we begin to build the kind of church that is in your song, it's going to take the hardest work some of us have ever had to do. It will take a commitment that none of us may have ever given to many efforts ever in our lives. But if you really want it, those are the things I promise you.

"However," Kyle paused to make sure the choir was listening, "you will have to make some promises to one another, too. What will those promises be?"

He listened to the whispers spreading through the room and watched the faces of all the well-intended people who were about to embark on the challenge of their lives, sparked by thoughts they may never have had before.

"I think we've had enough for one night. Think about what promises you are willing to make to one another and then to the rest of the congregation. That will be the subject of next week's meeting. I'll see you here at seven on the dot."

Insight 3: The second most important decision for a leader: What will you promise?

The second most important decision a leader must make is what he or she will promise to his or her people. For instance, Rev. Kyle made several promises to the choir, including a promise to lead them in having a great church.

A promise is not a claim, a theme, or a slogan. It is a personal pledge from the leader to everyone that he or she will help them be successful. The best promise a leader can make, to gain and keep a position of leadership, is to help his or her followers be successful in achieving what they want and need to achieve.

After the Meeting

Kyle left the room, but lingered in the hallway in case anyone wanted to discuss anything he had said. He knew that, in many cases, the most important part of a meeting was in its aftermath. That's when one found out if any of the seeds he or she had planted had taken root.

He heard muffled voices inside the room discussing what had transpired during the meeting. It was clear that the choir members were shocked with the promises he had made to them. But they seemed even more shocked that he had expected them to make promises to one another. He heard one choir member's voice above the crowd say, "Haven't all our years of singing together been sort of a promise? Why do we have to go out of our way to make promises to one another and the whole congregation now? What possible good could that do?"

Just as Kyle headed down the hall to his office, he heard the determined clicking of high heels coming from behind him.

"Wait, Rev. Martin. Do you have a minute?"

He turned around to see Susan O'Reilly, her pretty face flushed and her breathing winded. Susan had been a member of Community Church for only a couple of months after being away from Midville for years. He didn't know her whole story, just that she and her six-year-old son had moved back to live with her mother after Susan had gone through a very hurtful divorce.

"Hi, Susan. Did you need to talk about something?" Why did he feel like he was stuttering? And all of a sudden he was nervous. He had just faced a whole roomful of people, who wanted to see him publicly tarred and feathered, without a bit of nerves. Now, alone in this hallway with Susan, he felt like a schoolboy.

"Reverend, I'm not sure I agree with what you said about making promises."

"What do you mean?"

"Well, this may be my hang-up, but I've come to distrust promises and the people who make them. Promises are pretty bold statements. People come to count on those promises and then when they get broken—well, it just destroys confidence and hope and ... everything. Maybe it's better not to build up people's hopes too high. When you let them down, the hurt is really hard to take. You've got people really thinking in there. If they start believing in you and in this church and what we can become and then you let us down—it will hurt a lot more than if we had never listened to you ... never tried to make this church become better."

"Susan, you keep talking about the word *hurt*. Are you afraid that somehow being a part of all this will hurt you in some way?"

"Well, no … of course not. I just feel, I mean, *we* feel that making promises is risky. We can do a lot of exciting things here without making promises about how things will turn out. We don't need to give people unrealistic expectations."

"Realistic or unrealistic, causing people to have *great* expectations about what they can find at Community Church is the only way we will ever attract and keep anyone. I wouldn't want to belong to a church where the people weren't trying to create something special, something that people can rely on. I don't think you can do that without making promises to people. That's what commitment is all about."

"I know all about commitment…" Susan muttered.

Kyle turned momentarily to say good night to another member of the choir who was walking past him to the door. Then he turned back to respond to Susan, but she was gone.

Insight 4: Promises are vital, but extremely risky.

Promises are the key verses of any organization's song. You may not remember all the words of the song, but you always remember these verses. They are the heart-throbbing, toe-tapping parts of the music that sets one organization's song apart from another's. But promises are risky. They build up hope and expectations. Yet, without promises there is nothing special that compels people toward the organization or the people in it to believe in the organization's work and mission.

Susan's Home

Immediately upon stepping through the door, Susan was pummeled by a six-year-old ball of energy in footed pajamas, smelling delightfully of soap.

"Mommy, Mommy. I'm tho-o-o glad you're home," Zach said emphatically as he hugged her leg and grinned up at her. The two gaping holes where his front teeth had been made it difficult to pronounce his *s*'s, but it also made his face look even more disarming. His brown hair had been neatly combed to one side and was still slicked down from a very straight part—another clue that his bath had only been performed minutes before.

"How was your meeting? Was it in-ter-esting? Did you make a lot of de-ci-sions?" Susan knew Zach wasn't the least bit interested in her meeting, but it was a door opener and it was tactical. Zach always tried to engage her in conversation, on her turf, before he introduced the subject he really wanted to talk about.

So Susan played along as she gently guided her son back down the hallway to his room and then gave him the opening in the conversation that he was looking for.

"Yes, the meeting was very interesting, but that's not really what's on your mind, is it, young man?"

Zach liked it when she called him "young man." Sometimes it meant he was in trouble, but most of the time it meant that she thought he was growing up and that they could have "adult" conversations. Tonight, he could tell by the tone of things that he was on pretty solid ground to plead his case.

"Well, not 'xactly," Zach admitted. He now had the floor and wasn't going to give it up, so he just launched in. "Remember, when we first moved to Gram's and I was so sad, and you promised that when we got settled and everything, and if I was a really good boy, you would get me a new bike…? Well, Gram and me, we went out looking tonight and we found the bike! Oh, Mommy, it's so—bea-u-ti-ful! And it's *red*! Can I have it? *Pl-e-a-se*, can I? Gram said it wasn't *so* expensive and she said she would help. *Pl-e-a-se?*"

Susan looked at her son and wanted to cry. He was her whole world. Time seemed to stop as she tried to take in the entire wonder of him. She briefly glanced around the room, which was in an unusual state of order. Another not-so-subtle tactic, she mused. Even his motley collection of plastic dinosaurs was perfectly lined up on his windowsill: two T-Rexes, a Stegosaurus, and two Brontosauruses—or longnecks as he dubbed them.

"Did I *really* promise?" Susan asked knowingly.

"Yes, you *really* did … and you always said…"

"I know, 'A promise is a promise,' " Susan echoed. And then she thought fleetingly how odd it was that the word promise was used so frequently to define itself.

"Then I can have it? I can really have it?"

"You can, if you go to bed *right this minute.*" She watched her son scamper into his bed and pull up his covers.

Zach thought for a moment about asking for a story, but then changed his mind thinking he might be pressing his luck. Instead, he called out to his beautiful mother as she turned out the light, "Mommy, I'm really glad you had a good meeting!"

Susan resisted the urge to go back in and smother him with kisses and engage in a tickle fight. But she knew there would be no end to it if she did, and she was exhausted. She had a lot to think about—including how she was going to pay for the bike.

Instead she simply said, "I love you more than anything, Zach." She closed the door, leaving it open a small crack so that a thread of light landed on his smiling, contented face.

When Susan turned to go down the hall, she met her mother who had been eavesdropping.

"I'm glad you did it, Mom, don't worry. He deserves the bike, and I haven't had time to go looking for one."

Susan's mother, Marge, was relieved. It wasn't easy knowing where to step in and where to back off where her daughter and

Zach were concerned. Marge never minded taking care of him. And she was glad that Susan wanted to get out and start doing things again.

The divorce had been hard on Susan, and having to come back home and admit that she couldn't make it without help had been a bitter pill for her to swallow. Susan had been lucky though. There had been an opening in the public grade school, and they had put her to work the day after her interview.

At first Susan had joined Community because she believed Zach needed to be in Sunday school. That's the way she had been raised, and she was going to see to it that Zach had the same foundation. Without a father in his life, Zach was going to need all the stability he could get. She had hoped that Community Church could help fill in some gaps.

As for her own needs, she joined the choir so that she would have some adult companionship one night a week that would keep her mind off the blues. She also loved to sing and had, in fact, sung in the youth choir at Community when she was a girl. There was something about singing that set her free. But it was the joining of her voice with others to make a beautiful sound that was the real high for her. Two, ten, a hundred voices blended into one somehow made her feel powerful—all five feet, four inches of her.

On the other hand, solos weren't her cup of tea, never had been—not where singing was concerned and not in life, either. But it looked as if right now going solo was the way it was going to be for her. She would just have to accept that.

It would be a long time before she could trust anyone again. She wasn't even sure that time would ever come. That's why tonight's meeting had been particularly unnerving. She had been surprised by how easily she had gotten caught up in helping put together the song and the performance.

But now there were expectations, strings, and that awful word—*promises*. Why had she even bothered to go tonight?

Don, that's why. He had been a family friend for as long as she could remember. In fact, Don was the one who had gotten her involved with the choir again. So when he called her and told her how mad the minister had made him, she got mad too—mad enough to go and speak her piece.

Then that Rev. Kyle had to go and be—well—charming. He told them that they were right. He promised to help them create the best church possible. And he said he wouldn't leave until they kicked him out no matter how rough things got. But the worst part was, he expected them to make promises to one another and to the rest of the congregation. She didn't know if she was up to that.

All she wanted from the church right now was stability and support for Zach and, on occasion, a chance to sing with other people. A little companionship—nothing big—just a way to drive away those awful pangs of loneliness that would grip her in the middle of the night. If the church could promise her that, then that was enough.

As for what she could promise her friends at church—well at this moment—not a whole lot.

Insight 5: Promises are not always reciprocal.

People want and need promises from the organizations that are important to them, even if they, themselves, can promise nothing. For example, Susan joined Community Church for support during a difficult time in her life, but has expected nothing else and is unable to give anything back to the church.

The leader who makes promises, but who expects reciprocity from those being led, is in for major disappointment. People become a part of organizations for many different reasons. Some people want or expect very little from their institutions at first beyond the initial promise that the organization makes to be there for them. Therefore, it is up to the leader to try to raise the level of their involvement, commitment, and expectations for achievement.

The Parsonage

"**N**ot bad for a day's work…" Kyle said to himself.

The choir had gone from exhilarated to furious, from furious to questioning, from questioning to the beginnings of being "committed"—all within a short 24 hours.

That was the easy part.

The hard work, he knew, was ahead. Still, the right ingredients had been put into the pot, the heat had been turned up, and the soup was now beginning to boil.

He grabbed a soda out of the refrigerator and looked forward to watching a few innings of the baseball game and letting himself think about what he would do next. The baby-sitter had put the kids to bed early, so the house was quiet enough for him to reflect on the day.

But every time he started to think about the next step, his mind would wander back to Susan O'Reilly. He had to admit that he caught himself looking to see if Susan was at church on Sunday mornings, and he hung around doing necessary "catch up" paperwork at church on Wednesday evenings when the choir

practiced. So it was sheer pleasure when he turned and found
that it was Susan's high heels that had come tapping down the
hall after him that evening.

Since his wife had died, he hadn't felt the need for romantic
attachments. His two small children kept him busy enough—
and this new church was proving to be more than he could
handle. In his profession it seemed that he had to watch his
step with many of his female parishioners. There was always a
fine line between listening to problems and concerns and ...
well, he just wasn't good at it. It was also difficult to "date"
when you were in the ministry. Rumors spread easily and
quickly. Thinking otherwise was a great way to lose your job.
So he found it easier to not even think of having a relationship
and to protect his back—at least it was until recently.

For some reason this woman made him want a lot more. It
made him both sad and furious to know that someone had made
her afraid to make promises, or hear them, and to worry about
those who counted on the promises that were made. He
wondered how many of the other choir members had similar
reasons to be afraid. If the choir couldn't make promises, then
it would be impossible for the rest of the congregation.

Come to think of it, he mused, until today how many significant
promises had *he* made in his lifetime?

He would think about that one later.

Insight 6: Almost everyone fears making promises, which is why making them is such a compelling act for an individual and an organization.

Though Rev. Kyle made several promises to the choir, Susan and the other choir members were afraid to make promises to him or to the church. It's paradoxical that while we often try to get others to make promises to us, almost everyone has some fear making promises. That's why so few are made. It is also the reason that making promises is such a compelling act for an individual and an organization.

The Next Meeting

This time Kyle made sure he was on time—seven o'clock sharp. When he entered the room it was already abuzz with good-natured conversation and laughter, but the room quieted quickly with his presence in it.

It was clear that the choir was still not sure what kind of person their minister was or what they could expect from him. That was all very understandable. So Kyle thought he would try to ease their discomfort by being upbeat and direct. "How'd you do with the promises?"

Silence.

"Well, I can see I was a big hit last week. Yet, you are all here. You must have *something* you want to say…."

A voice from the back answered his question. It was Irv Finkbinder, one of the more outspoken participants from the previous meeting. Perhaps somewhere along the line Irv had found his voice and liked the sound of it. "We've all been talking. It was pretty hard for us to come up with what we could promise, so we started with the things we would like to count on the church for, and we thought maybe that would give us an idea of what we could promise each other."

"Ok, Irv, that sounds like a good idea. Why don't you share your list, and I'll put the ideas on this flipchart."

Irv began and Kyle wrote. Their expectations ran the full gamut from small to large, from the easily doable to the time and resource intensive. But most of the ideas and expectations were terrific. Irv wanted a support group for widowers and a full-time pre-school for his grandchildren. Tony Coffman wanted the church to run a food bank. And Martha Scully wanted a gym, aerobics, and weight-loss classes, and she saw no reason why the church couldn't be a place where people could go for these things.

Every so often another member of the choir would stop Irv to clarify a point or add to it with a personal anecdote. It became evident that the list had truly been a collaboration, and everyone was highly invested in it. Except for one. Susan was in a chair off from the others, and she looked deeply disturbed.

"Susan, we haven't heard from you yet. It might be nice to get the impressions of someone who used to belong, left, and then came back," Kyle offered hopefully.

"Well, I…." Her back stiffened, and he could see the walls go up slowly and deliberately. "If you don't mind I'd rather just observe for awhile."

"That's not like you," Irv proclaimed as he came forward looking very much like he was going to hug her. "You always have a lot to add." Irv was truly having a glory moment and he couldn't stand the thought of anyone not enjoying it as much as he was.

"Irv, please. I would just like to listen to the rest of you if you don't mind," Susan responded, hoping he would just let her go back to being invisible. Her hands were nervously fidgeting with a rubber band she had found on the floor. She looked down as her eyes began filling up with tears. She desperately wanted the focus to be *off* of her. All of a sudden she felt like she could barely breathe.

Martha decided to rescue her, "I have something to add…"

The diversion worked, and everyone was back to business again.

Susan let out a sigh of relief and continued to study these people whom she sang with every week. They all had a past. All of them were the result of their hurts, their joys, their fears, their disappointments, their hopes, and their needs. They all needed something from Community. And maybe she did too. But she sure wasn't going to express it here—in front of everyone.

It took a whole hour and many pieces of paper until a full list of hopes and expectations were recorded. When they were done, the choir felt spent, but satisfied. The process somehow had a healing quality to it that no one had expected to feel.

These were people who had been together every Wednesday night and Sunday morning for more years than anyone could count, but until now they had never shared what they really wanted and needed out of their church. No wonder the idea of making promises to one another was so foreign to them.

Before tonight, they didn't know enough about what one another wanted or needed to understand what promises to make or how to fulfill them.

Kyle closed the meeting this way: "You have done a remarkable job tonight. I think it is safe to say that the hopes and expectations that you have shared represent many of the hopes and expectations of the rest of the congregation." As he looked around the room he could see heads nod in easy agreement.

"Now for your assignment for next week…" Audible groans and then chuckling bubbled up from the choir. "What are your *ideas* for making these expectations a reality here at Community? See you next week—same time."

The Crisis

Susan was lagging behind her fellow choir members as they filed out of the meeting room, when her cell phone rang. Fumbling through her purse to find her phone, she edged her way back to the corner of the room where she would be better able to hear.

Kyle had been watching Susan, hoping to find an excuse to steal a few moments alone with her, so he was the first to see her collapse into a chair, her face contorted with alarm and her free hand tugging nervously on her hair. "When?" "Where?" and "Is he all right?" were the only phrases Kyle could make out over the din of the choir's still lively chatting.

Suddenly, and without reservation he found himself at Susan's side, wanting to relieve her of whatever had caused her so much pain.

"What's wrong? What can I do?" he pleaded.

"It's my son… I've got to get to the hospital…" Susan was suddenly out of her mind. She couldn't even look at Kyle. She just stood up and tried to make her way out of the room.

She could barely breathe, and she couldn't feel her legs moving under her. All she knew was that she had to get to the hospital. People—there were people everywhere—they were all in her way, slowing her down!

"Please, I've got to get out of here," she moaned as she clawed her way through the crowded hallway.

Kyle ran after her, grabbed her by the arm and steered her through the mob. "I don't know what's going on, but I do know that you are in no condition to drive," he said. "I'm going to take you to the hospital, and I don't want you to argue with me."

She didn't argue.

As soon as Kyle got her seated in his truck, she started to cry.

"He just has to be all right... He just has to be..." she said as she sat rocking in her seat, arms crossed in front of her and her hands gripping her shoulders.

"After all we've been through, I just can't lose him." Susan was talking to herself now.

Kyle was already speeding down the highway toward the hospital when he finally asked, "What happened? You've got to tell me."

In a broken voice Susan started to explain, "That was my mom on the phone. Zach was hit by a car! My mom was hysterical so that's all I know. I don't even know if he's alive or dead!

Rev. Kyle, I don't know if I can handle this. If I lose Zach I don't know what I will do. He's the best thing that's ever happened to me." Susan was sobbing uncontrollably.

Kyle pulled up to the emergency entrance, jumped out of the truck, and raced around the other side to help Susan out.

"Well, I can tell you this. I promise you won't have to go through any of this alone."

In the Hospital

The minute Kyle and Susan stepped through the doors to the emergency room, they were met by Susan's mother, Marge, and a man named Ward Holiday, who was also a member of Community Church. Their faces were racked with guilt and pain. But it was Ward who was the first one to speak. "Miss O'Reilly, I didn't see your son coming. All of a sudden he just appeared on his bike from behind a parked car, I couldn't brake soon enough… There aren't words…"

Marge interrupted, "I just ran into the house for a minute. The phone rang—I know I should have just let it ring, but I…"

"Where is he? Is he going to be OK?" Susan asked, struggling to hold herself together. She was so scared, and she knew she couldn't bear it if they told her Zach was gone. So she held her breath while she listened to her mother.

"He's in the operating room. Honey, he's hurt really bad."

Her mother tried to hug her, but Susan shrugged her off. She didn't want to be comforted. She didn't want to be here. She just wanted to collect her son and go home. This wasn't happening. It couldn't be happening.

Susan looked around for a place where she could be alone. But the emergency waiting room was small and there were no hiding places to be had.

Then she heard the outside doors burst open, and there were Don Wilson and his wife. A moment later Tony Coffman, Irv Finkbinder, and Martha Scully appeared. More people crowded in—the whole choir. Before she could escape, she was being smothered in the hugs that she had tried to deny from her mother just moments before. People with tears in their eyes were telling her that they just knew Zach was going to pull through. While the faces were blurring together, she felt herself yield to the hope they were desperately trying to give her.

And then the vigil began. The hours ticked by, and the coffee, no matter how many times it was freshly brewed, tasted bitter and stale in the wee hours of the morning.

Most of the choir had left by now, but Rev. Kyle had stayed. As had her mother and Ward and Irv. The emotions in the small room made the waiting time even more difficult. Both her mother and Ward were trying to keep themselves together emotionally, even while their worry and guilt was making them physically sick. The thick, black coffee that they kept pouring into small, Styrofoam cups and drinking nervously wasn't helping things either.

Susan was huddled in a corner of the room away from the others, trying to brace herself for the worst—if the surgeon came through the door with the news that Zach hadn't made it. The choir's flood of hugs and attention had been surprisingly comforting to her, but now that they were gone, the anguish she felt was taking over once again.

Finally, the double doors that led to the operating room swung open, and a very tired-looking doctor in green scrubs asked which one of the worried people in the waiting room was Mrs. O'Reilly.

Susan immediately stood, her legs wobbly, her stomach churning.

The doctor came to her and took her hands. "It was a very tough operation, a skull fracture and four broken bones. He will need a lot of physical therapy, and we are not out of the woods yet, but I think Zach will pull through…."

When she heard "physical therapy," all Susan could think was, "That means he's alive! I can deal with anything as long as he's alive."

"Doctor, you've got to tell me he *will* pull through. You've got to *promise* me that he will. He's all I've got. He's my whole life. You've just got to promise me," Susan pleaded.

The doctor looked at her with the compassion of a man who was by now almost as involved in Zach's well being as she was. "Mrs. O'Reilly, nothing would give me more pleasure than to make you that promise, but there are some things that are out of my control. What I can promise you is that I will do everything in my power to help him pull through, and so will everyone on the staff at this hospital. He's a hearty little boy. His chances are better then most."

Susan had tears in her eyes now, knowing that she would have to hold on to the hope that the doctor was offering her. Finally, she looked him in the eyes and said, "Thank you for that. Thank you very much for that…."

Insight 7: There is always a promise we can make.

Even when promises are difficult to make, people still want and need us to make them. There are, of course, promises we cannot make, because they are not within our total power and control to ensure that they are kept. However, there is always some promise that we can make. Trying our very best on someone's behalf is one of those promises. For instance, the doctor promised Susan that he would do whatever he can to improve Zach's chances, without promising that Zach will pull through— a promise he can't necessarily keep.

A Return to Normalcy

One of the great truisms of life is that it goes on—no matter what tragedies occur in the middle of it.

And so it was for life at Community Church. The parishioners had, of course, all heard about Susan and Zach and Marge and Ward Holiday, and most had gone out of their way to offer their support, their help, and their concern. Zach had regained consciousness, though he was in a great deal of pain. Nonetheless, people became absorbed once again in their own problems and their own concerns.

So when Monday night rolled around, and it was time for the choir to meet to discuss their ideas for making their expectations of the church a reality, everyone was there, ready for their next round of discovery. Surprisingly, many of the choir members had arrived with written lists.

Once again Kyle was ready with a flipchart and a new box of markers.

Right out of the chute, Irv Finkbinder piped up, "I'm very sorry that this thing happened to Zach O'Reilly. But, I have to say it's really got me thinking. I heard the surgeon make a promise to a person he'd never even seen before that he would do everything he could on behalf of her little boy. I also saw how important it was at that moment to Susan that he make her that promise.

"I've done a one-eighty on this idea of making promises. The church *has* to be a place where people can feel supported when something horrible happens. This accident didn't just hurt Zach. It hurt Susan's mother, Marge, and Ward and Susan and everyone who cares about them. The church has to promise to be there for them…. Rev. Kyle, put that up as the first item on the flipchart."

Before Kyle could begin writing, Martha Scully interrupted, "I agree with you Irv, but I also don't think we're being totally honest. We've all known what Rev. Kyle has been trying to tell us all along. We just didn't want to admit it until now because what he is asking us to do is hard.

"People want the church to be there for them, but how do they *know* it will be. What can we put in place that will help us make good on the promise that it will be there when people need it? A lot of churches make claims. What we want is a church that goes beyond claims—beyond platitudes."

At first the room was silent. People were pondering what Martha had just said. Then Don declared, "Oh my gosh, Reverend—that's what you meant when you said that our song was 'a real *feel good* experience.'

"What you meant was that unless we made promises with concrete ideas and then carried out those ideas—all we had was a *one-time* feel good experience… Well I'll be damned! I mean darned," he added sheepishly.

"Damned or darned, you're both right on target." Kyle was beaming. These people were amazing. He never expected them to get it so quickly. He would certainly never underestimate them again. Don, Martha, and Irv had put it together, just as they had with their song. No one could have put it more eloquently. These people were the salt of the earth, and he felt privileged to be a part of them.

He wished Susan were there. He missed her. He had been with her every day since the accident, and it seemed as if she was beginning to trust him. In fact, it was starting to be more than that, he was sure of it. But there was no doubt that Susan O'Reilly was not a person who would open herself up easily to any human being at this stage in her life. If only she could witness what her friends in the choir were starting to discover about themselves and about the church, Kyle thought wistfully. Maybe then she would understand that these were people who wanted to make good on their promises and who were going to work very hard to do so.

"Hey, Reverend, snap out of it!" Martha announced boldly. "We've got a lot of work to do. Most of us came with some pretty long lists of what we'd like to see happen around here. So you better get writing!"

"Sorry, Martha. At your service!" Kyle saluted her. "Just start shouting out the ideas and I'll write as fast as I can," he said with a smile. Martha was a bossy one, Kyle thought to himself. But as long as the Marthas of the church were in the middle of things, the church would move light years forward. No, a good straw boss was what the choir needed, and she was a good one.

An hour and a half later, his arm and wrist aching, Kyle announced that they had twenty-two promises and one hundred and fifty-eight ideas of how to implement those promises.

Everyone in the room was bone tired, but exhilarated at the same time.

"Now, I think we're ready," Kyle summed up, laying down the beleaguered marker.

"Ready for what?" Tony Coffman asked expectantly. He was itching to take these ideas for a test drive and was hoping that was what Rev. Kyle was going to say next.

"It's time we got the rest of the church involved in what we're thinking and see if we can make an impression on anyone."

"With all due respect, Reverend," Martha interjected, "the people in this choir have been the only ones who could be counted on to do anything around here. I think we're wasting our time on the other members until *we,* ourselves, get some things going."

"You may be right, Martha, but we have to try," Kyle retorted. "This church isn't going to be all it can be with the participation of the choir alone. We need the ideas and the actions of as many people as possible."

"What do you have in mind?" Tony offered, hoping to diffuse Martha and give Kyle the backing he needed to rally the rest of the people in the church to action.

"I think we ought to publish our list of promises and ideas to the entire congregation. Then we should invite them to a meeting where they can add to this list with a list of their own and see where it takes us," Kyle answered with resolve.

"Great idea!" Irv said enthusiastically.

"I think you are all nuts," Martha countered, "but, I'm game. What do you need me to do, Reverend?"

"Martha, I was afraid you'd never ask," Kyle said laughingly. And the meeting ended with everyone chuckling as Martha appointed herself to organize and chair the meeting.

> **Insight 8: The third most important decision for a leader: Finding and developing the right ideas that will help people and the organization find success.**
>
> *The third most important decision every leader must make is to decide what ideas he or she will embrace to give concrete legs to his or her leadership. Ideas are the notes, the instruments, and the musicians that an organization uses to build and play its song. Without these key components there is no music, only words. The words may be eloquent, but they carry no melody alone. Without practical and workable ideas, the mission of the organization isn't heard or believed. It falls on deaf ears.*

By no means do all the ideas of the organization have to emanate from the leader. In fact, the more ideas that can come from the group being led, the better. But it is the leaders' job to see that as many people are involved in the process as possible. And it is also the leader's job to help make good ideas become practical realities. For example, Rev. Kyle brings the choir together to develop ideas and concrete plans to improve the church before addressing the entire congregation.

If people knew how to be successful, they would be, but many don't know how. It takes good ideas to make people and the organization find success. It takes positive and constructive ideas to cause people to accept you, believe in you, be jolted out of their fears and indifference, and follow your leadership. And without these ideas for creating success, there can be no plan or achievement.

The Day of the Big Meeting

Two weeks had passed, and every day Kyle spent at least one hour with Martha Scully, at her request, plotting and planning the meeting with the entire congregation.

Kyle hadn't anticipated the level of detail that Martha would feel was required to pull off the meeting successfully. There were announcements to be made, bulletins to be written and distributed, formal invitations to be issued, and refreshments to be decided on and served.

Kyle found himself wondering if his original thought about the need for "a good straw boss" was a sound one. And yet he had to admit he had complete confidence that Martha would leave no stone unturned to produce a successful meeting, even if she had to call every member of the congregation herself.

Don proudly posted the sign outside the church which said:

```
Meeting Monday
At 7:00 p.m.
The Rebirth of Community Church
We have promises we want to make to you.
Please come.
```

The original list of promises and ideas for implementation were put in an expanded church bulletin with an invitation to come to the meeting. Martha didn't make all the phone calls herself after all. Rather, she organized scores of volunteers to make personal phone calls to see to it that there was a decent crowd.

Still, on the day of the meeting, she came to Kyle and said, "Reverend, I've done everything I know how to do, but I still can't be sure anybody but the choir members are going to show up tonight. Please don't be too disappointed if you have to admit that I was right all along. I still think the choir may be the only people who are really interested. It's just the way it is."

"Ye of little faith, Martha. Actually, you've done a great job, and I think you're the one who's going to be disappointed if the crowd isn't what you've worked for." In truth, Kyle was just about to admit to Martha that he was a little skeptical himself, when the phone rang.

It was Susan. "Kyle, you have to come right away. Zach's taken a turn for the worse. Please, you've just got to come."

"I'm leaving right now. Hang on. I'll be right there."

Kyle looked around his office frantically for the keys to his truck.

"What is it Reverend?" Martha demanded. "What's happened?"

"It's Zach. Susan says something's gone wrong. That's all I know. Martha, you may have to handle the meeting yourself tonight." And he was out the door.

Back at the Hospital

Kyle's truck screeched to a stop in front of the emergency entrance. He bolted from the truck and through the first set of doors. An enthusiastic teenage girl in a red and white striped uniform met him and said, "In the surgery waiting room, Reverend, follow the hallway and turn left, you'll run right into it. Mrs. O'Reilly's pretty shook up."

"Thanks, Rebecca." Kyle recognized her from the church youth group, but said no more and raced down the hall.

When he got to the surgery waiting room, Susan flew into his arms crying. "Kyle, everything was going so well, and then Zach just slipped into a coma. The doctor's not sure, but they think it's a blood clot. I'm so scared…"

He hugged her and as he did he could feel her own grip on him become tighter. And then slowly, as the sobbing subsided he could feel her begin to relax. "Susan, I'm going to stay here with you—whatever happens, for as long as it takes. How long's Zach been in the operating room?"

"They took him in right before I called you. They said it would be hours before we knew anything—that is if he makes it that far. Kyle, I was just beginning to believe that our lives might be OK again."

Kyle didn't say anything. He simply pulled her to him on the couch, hunkering in for a long wait.

She pulled away momentarily and looked at him with a sudden realization. "But tonight's your meeting. You can't stay here. You've got to be at the church."

"Martha's got it covered. Anyway, as much as I'd like to think otherwise, I'm not fooling myself. It'll probably be just the choir members who show up. "

Susan was strangely calm. The weeks of wrestling with the problems of Zach's condition had given her a newfound strength—albeit sometimes fleeting. She looked up at Kyle and said, "You're wrong about what's happening at Community Church, Kyle. People are getting *engaged* again. Everyone feels it. *I* was even planning to come to tonight's meeting."

"It would be nice if you were right, but you have more important things to think about right now. Why don't you close your eyes and try to relax. I'm not going anywhere."

Susan tried to let herself relax against him. She wanted to believe that everything would be okay. That Zach would make it. And that she could perhaps even think about having a new life with this surprising man who sat beside her. But every time she began to think that way, the horror of what could happen if she lost Zach jolted her back into reality.

Then her mother came into the waiting room, followed closely by Ward Holiday. Susan sat up stiffly. How did they know about Zach anyway? Susan was so upset she had only called Kyle.

"Martha called," Marge said, answering the question that was in her daughter's eyes. "Don't be surprised if the whole choir shows up here. You know Martha. Have you heard anything yet?"

"No, Mom. But as long as they're in there, there's hope. It means that he is still...."

"Don't even say it. Zach's a strong kid, he's going to pull through," Marge offered, as if saying the words would make it true.

She reached out for Susan's hand and this time, thankfully, it wasn't rejected. The past few weeks had been some of the hardest she and Susan had ever shared together. Marge knew that Susan was trying not to blame her for the accident, but she also knew that Susan couldn't help herself. And Marge knew that if the roles had been reversed she would have felt the same way. Susan had left her in charge. That it was an accident didn't change the fact that because of her negligence, Zach might die.

If it hadn't been for her friends at church, Marge wouldn't have been able to make it through the difficulty of the past weeks. The women in the auxiliary had listened to her, had comforted her, and had offered her simple companionship that somehow gave her hope and strength. At the same time, she found herself listening to them. Each took her turn and had shared her own story. Each had a son, a sister, or a friend that was dealing with an illness, a struggling business, or a failed relationship. It was as if these experiences shared among people who cared about one another somehow built a resiliency in all of them. Ward's wife was in the church auxiliary as well. Even she and Marge had forged a friendship as they tried to help each other cope.

Ward had had a similar experience with the men's group. The men had rallied around him in wave after wave of unanimous support. They neither judged him nor told him what to do. They listened to him, took him to the local ball games, included him in their golf outings, and asked him to join them when they went for coffee at the local coffee shop.

Ward's two children were in the youth group and were friends of Rebecca, the candy striper at the hospital. They relied on Rebecca for their daily news about Zach's condition since it had become a subject to avoid asking about at home.

Marge was suddenly very aware of the interesting fabric that the church had helped weave during this crisis.

Even Susan was now different. A month ago she had acted cut off and guarded with her closest friends. Now Marge could see the hard edges crumbling. The Susan that was emerging was somehow softer and more trusting—vulnerable.

Steadily, the waiting room began to fill up—first with Marge's friends from the woman's auxiliary. Then, Ward's friends from the men's group came in with their wives.

Next, Susan's colleagues from school began to pour into the hospital. Then, Zach's friends and their parents arrived. And of course, the choir, the always-steadfast choir—Tony Coffman, Irv Finkbinder, and Martha Scully leading the pack.

Susan was overcome. There were people everywhere—sitting on the floor, leaning against the walls of the hallway, spilling out of the waiting room. And more were filtering in by the minute. At first there was only the sound of muffled whispers, but as more and more people came in, the room seemed to be bursting with noise.

Marge was the first to speak up. "Wasn't there supposed to be a meeting tonight? Shouldn't you all be there?" she asked in disbelief.

Then she saw Don making his way through the crowd. He yelled, "I put up a sign that said the meeting was cancelled 'cause Zach was in trouble. Guess everybody decided to come down here!"

Martha came over to Susan, put her hand on her shoulder, and said, "Susan, everyone wanted to be here. We may not know anything about building a church, but we know a lot about what it means to be there for someone who needs us."

At that moment the doctor came out of the operating room pulling the green scrub cap off of his head, wiping his brow with his forearm. He surveyed the crowd. His eyes finally found Susan and he started to speak. At once the room was silent.

"Susan, you've got one tough little boy there. He'll be in the ICU for the next few days. But he's going to be OK."

A cheer went up from the crowd, and everyone in the room started hugging one another. Ward sank down in a chair and sobbed, as did Marge.

Susan turned to Kyle and hugged him too. "Thanks for being here, Kyle… I couldn't have made it…"

Kyle silenced her by putting two fingers lightly on her mouth and saying, "I told you I wasn't going anywhere, and I'm not."

"But your meeting… Kyle, the meeting was so important."

"I told you, you have more important things to think about," Kyle said softly.

Then Martha, never one to pass up an opportunity, yelled across the room, "We've got everyone we need. Why don't we just have the meeting here?"

Irv chimed in, "I hate to admit it, but she's right. There are still people parking their cars and coming in. They read Don's sign, but they still want a meeting. I think most of the church is here. In fact, there are a lot of people who don't even belong to Community that are here."

"I don't get it…" Kyle trailed off.

"Hey, Reverend, we want to hear more about these promises and your ideas. And we have a few of our own to add, if you don't mind," an unfamiliar voice resounded from the back of the room.

Not wasting any time, Martha cleared the magazines off of the coffee table in a single, magnificent gesture. Then pounding her rather weighty handbag on the table top she declared, "This meeting of the NEW Community Church is now called to order!"

"Wait a minute folks," the doctor bellowed. "I don't want to throw cold water on what I'm sure is a very important meeting," he gave Martha a reassuring look that took the heat out of her face, "but you can't meet here. There are people who will need this waiting room tonight. Besides it's too small. Why don't you go to the cafeteria?"

That's all Martha needed. "To the cafeteria then!" she commanded, and she led the throng of people who chattered away with their friends about the events of this remarkable evening.

And so the meeting proceeded. It was a wonderful cacophony of ideas, emotions, stories of the experiences members had had at Community Church, and expressed desires of what they wanted it to be in the future. They reminisced, they laughed and, best of all, when it was over there were two tablets full of ideas that these good people wanted to carry out. Rebecca had offered to stay and act as the scribe, with the condition that she was allowed to organize the youth committee to tackle some of the ideas *she* had for the church.

After the last ideas were being recorded and people were
getting up to leave, Kyle stood up and addressed the group that
remained, "I've just got one question. Why now? Why did this
happen here tonight?"

Ward offered boldly, "It's pretty simple, Reverend. No one ever
promised us anything before.

"I've got to admit, I was pretty skeptical at first. Words can be
meaningless. But I sure wanted to believe what I was starting
to hear from people like Irv, Tony, and Don. We need a church
we can rely on. I've been miserable in these last weeks since
the accident, but you and the others in this church were there
for me. I'll never forget it and neither will my family. Tony
and Don have been telling me that you're for real. I know now
that they're right."

As Irv listened to Ward's statement he began to hum. At first it
was hard to discern *what* he was humming. But then a few of
the other choir members picked up on the tune and began to
hum as well. Slowly, the melody became louder and more
deliberate as other voices joined in. Then, in unison, a few of
the choir members began singing the words. Soon everyone in
the room was humming, singing, swaying, or clapping.

It wasn't just *a* song. It was *the* song. THEIR SONG. The
song that had inspired a minister and now an entire
congregation to grow to another level of understanding about
what they could achieve together.

They sang it differently than they had a month ago. This
time it was not just a *feel good* experience. It had the

richness and body of a sound that came out of people who had grown into it, had grown through it, had incorporated other voices with it, and had lived it. It was a song that would soon have many verses, but the refrain would always be the same—powerful, compelling, inspiring.

As the music began to die down, a man rose slowly from the center of the room. "I'm not a member of Community Church," he said quietly, "but you can bet I'm going to be after tonight. I work here at the hospital and was just getting off my shift when I saw all these people in the cafeteria. Curiosity got the better of me, and I just had to find out what was going on. I'm new to town and our family has been looking for a church that we can feel part of. Then I saw my neighbor, Tony, here. He's been telling me about what was happening at the church, so I thought I'd stay to see if what he was saying was true. I've got to tell you, I wasn't expecting much, but you people have changed my mind about what a church can be. Now, I just want to know how I can help make your list of ideas happen."

It was Irv who spoke first. "Do you sing? The choir's always looking for another voice."

The gentle laughter that followed and the handshakes and words of welcome made this newcomer know that he had found a home.

Insight 9: People are compelled toward people and institutions that promise to be their advocates—and don't leave them easily.

Most people don't have that many people or institutions they can count on to be totally committed to their welfare. When they find one, they are compelled to follow and support that person or institution.

People don't leave advocates, they leave enemies. When a leader and the institution decide to become the total advocate for the constituency and openly and freely tell them by word and deed that the institution is an advocate, the organization will experience exponential growth.

Epilogue

Kyle had risen early and had arrived at the church before the first citizens of Midville had begun to stir. Now, from the front steps of the church, he looked out over this wonderful little town. "It must have rained last night," he said to himself wistfully. The morning rays of light were dancing on the puddles in the street. It promised to be a beautiful day, and he breathed it in like a man reborn.

There was a tremendous amount of work to be done, but he knew that after last night it would all begin to fall into place. Zach had regained consciousness a few hours after everyone had gone home. Kyle and Zach had even shared a few knock-knock jokes before Zach fell asleep. And tonight Kyle was having dinner, alone, with Susan. That was enough to put any red-blooded man in a good mood.

Martha Scully had volunteered to work half days to get all the new ideas of the church off the ground. And with the new light of day, Kyle felt that he was even up to handling Martha. Yes, things were looking up for him and Community Church.

Yet, as he looked back on all the things that had happened in the last month, he realized that it was he, himself, who had been the most transformed. He had gone from cynic to cheerleader, from skeptic to full-fledged believer—a believer in what good people could do, could forgive, could be, could overcome. He also knew that life with these people would never be the same. They would be pushing him—hard. But that was better than pulling them any day of the week. No, there would be no resting on his laurels now. The song, his conviction, and the people of Community had changed all that.

He could hardly wait to get started.

Questions for Discussion

To think more deeply about the 9 insights...

- Insight 1: The potential of an organization's song is great, but it is just that—*potential.*
- Insight 2: Your most important decision: How will you position yourself as the leader?
- Insight 3: The second most important decision for a leader: What will you promise?
- Insight 4: Promises are vital, but extremely risky.
- Insight 5: Promises are not always reciprocal.
- Insight 6: Almost everyone fears making promises, which is why making them is such a compelling act for an individual and an organization.
- Insight 7: There is always a promise we can make.
- Insight 8: The third most important decision for a leader: Finding and developing the right ideas that will help people and the organization find success.
- Insight 9: People are compelled toward people and institutions that promise to be their advocates—and don't leave them easily.

...the following questions are helpful discussion starters:

1. What is your organization's song? What is your own individual tune within the organization? Is it consistent with the organization's song? In other words, do you provide a good harmony or melody for the institution, or are you singing off key?

2. As a leader, how have you decided to position yourself? Will you be a leader who will allow things to materialize in their own way, or will you be a leader

who will cause things to happen? Will you be a leader who seizes opportunities and makes the most of them, or one that lets opportunities slip by? Will you be one who will settle for a good organization, or will you take every action you can to make your organization great? What other ways can you think of to position yourself as a leader?

3. As a leader, what promises are you willing to make to the people you are trying to lead? What promises do people want you to make? What gets in the way of your making promises to people? How might your leadership become more compelling if you decided to make promises to people—and to keep them?

4. What promises do you want the important institutions in your life to make to you? What would you do for an institution or person who kept these promises?

5. As a leader, what are your ideas for ensuring the success of the organization, the people in it, and the people the institution serves? How can you get more ideas?

6. Are you a total advocate for the people you are trying to lead? How do you fall down from time to time in your advocacy? What could happen if the customers or clients of your organization felt that your organization was *their* total advocate?

When the Choir Began to Sing is the preceding book to *The Power of the Song*.

When the Choir Began to Sing offers the following insights:

- Insight 1: The "choir" is an untapped source of power for leaders.
- Insight 2: Even when change is positive, we need to grieve what was lost.
- Insight 3: Unresolved problems become unintended consequences.
- Insight 4: Identifying the problem is half the battle.
- Insight 5: People don't like being forced to change.
- Insight 6: There is a leader within each of us waiting to make a difference.
- Insight 7: Urgency focuses energy and drives change.
- Insight 8: The "choir" is our connection to the rest of the world.
- Insight 9: The more power you give away, the more you get back.
- Insight 10: Preach to the choir ... but in the right way.
- Insight 11: When you are on the right path, you end up where you want to be.

To order this book, simply call The MASTER Teacher at 1-800-669-9633 or visit www.masterteacher.com.